Piano Accompaniment

Play the Great Masters!

18 Favorite Classics for Young Players

Arranged by
James Curnow

Order Number: CMP 1069-06-401

Arranged by James Curnow
Play The Great Masters
Piano Accompaniment

ISBN-10: 90-431-2412-5
ISBN-13: 978-90-431-2412-6

James Curnow

James Curnow was born in Port Huron, Michigan and raised in Royal Oak, Michigan. His formal training was received at Wayne State University (Detroit, Michigan) and at Michigan State University (East Lansing, Michigan), where he was a euphonium student of Leonard Falcone, and a conducting student of Dr. Harry Begian. James Curnow has taught in all areas of instrumental music, both on the public school, and college and university level.

James Curnow has become one of the world's most prolific writers for concert, brass bands and orchestra. He has been commissioned to compose over one-hundred works for band and various ensembles. Curnow's published works now number well over four hundred. Averaging eight to ten commissions a year, of which at least four are major works, Curnow's music is performed all over the world.

Available Books:

Flute/Oboe - CMP 1078-06-400

Clarinet - CMP 1070-06-400

Alto/Baritone Saxophone CMP 1071-06-400

Soprano/Tenor Saxophone - CMP 1072-06-400

Trumpet - CMP 1073-06-400

F/E♭ Horn - CMP 1074-06-400

Bassoon/Trombone/Euphonium BC/TC - CMP 1075-06-400

Piano Accompaniment - CMP 1069-06-401

Play The Great Masters!

Franz Peter Schubert (1797-1828) - Marche Militaire
Born in Vienna, Austria as the youngest child of four sons, he and his brothers grew up assisting their father in school teaching duties. A prolific composer, he is best known for his lieder (Art songs).

Engelbert Humperdinck (1854 -1921) - Suite From Hansel And Gretel
Hailed by Richard Wagner as his heir apparent, he was born in Siegburg, Germany and died in Neustrelitz. His compositional output was small but his opera, Hansel and Gretel, from which these two pieces are taken, was a tremendous success.

Franz Joseph Haydn (1732-1809) - Serenade Opus 3, No. 5
Franz Joseph Haydn was an illustrious Austrian composer, the first master of Viennese Classicism, and the "Father of the Symphony", of which he wrote over one hundred. This melody became the Austrian national anthem.

Antonin Dvorak (1854-1904) - Slavonic Dances Opus 72, No. 3
Antonin Dvorak was a Czechoslovakian composer who played violin and organ, and through his music, established a strong Czech Nationalistic style. From 1892 to 1895, he spent time in the United States as a composition teacher and director of the National Conservatory of Music in New York. During this time, he composed his Symphony #9, "From the New World", from which this theme has been extracted.

Johannes Brahms (1833-1897) - Waltz
Johannes Brahms was born in Hamburg and died in Vienna. He was considered to be one of the greatest German composers. He was a master symphonist of the late Romantic period and composed significant works for voice, piano, orchestra, and various small ensembles.

Edward A. MacDowell (1860-1908) - To A Wild Rose
This American composer was born in New York and after studying abroad returned to the United States where he taught, performed (piano) and conducted until his death in that same city. He is best remembered for his piano works.

Franz Peter Schubert (1797-1828) - Sanctus
See biography above.
Schubert's beautiful chorale Sanctus (Holy, Holy, Holy) is part of his much revered German Mass in F.

Edvard Grieg (1843-1907) - In The Hall Of The Mountain King
From Peer Gynt Suite No. 1
Born in Bergen, Norway he was an internationally recognized pianist and composer and was one of the first Norwegian composers to seek to create a truly national Norwegian music, which included the use of Norwegian folk songs.

George Bizet (1838-1875) - Habanera from Carmen
A French composer, he is best remembered for his large scale operas. Habanera (a Spanish dance) is from his most successful opera-comique, Carmen, composed in 1874.

Peter Ilyich Tchaikovsky (1840-1894) - Andante From Piano Concerto No. 1
Considered to be one of the "Mighty Five" Russian composers, he was born in Viatka Province, Western Central Urals and died in St. Petersburg. A composer who wrote in all forms of music but excelled, he is most revered for his large scale orchestral works.

Alexander Porfiryevich Borodin (1833-1887) - Theme from String Quartet #2 "Nocturne"
Also one of the "Mighty Five" Russian composers, Borodin (born and died in St. Petersburg, Russia) is known for only a handful of works: 2 lyrical string quartets (String Quartet #2 being the composition from which the Nocturne (Night Song) is extracted), three symphonies and his exotic work Prince Igor.

Frederic Chopin (1810-1849) - Polonaise Op. 53
Incomparable Polish composer and genius of the piano, Chopin created created a unique romantic style of keyboard music. He was basically self-taught but extremely dedicated and committed to the piano.

Johann Strauss, Jr. (1825-1899) - The Blue Danube Waltz
This greatly renowned Austrian violinist, composer, conductor, and son of Johann Strauss Sr. is known as "The Waltz King". His waltz, Blue Danube (actual title: On the Beautiful Blue Danube) caused a great sensation and had critics raving that it was "the waltz of all waltzes."

Jaques Offenbach (1819-1880) - Can Can

Born in Cologne, Germany but considered a French composer, he was raised and resided in Paris until he death there in 1880. Although heavily criticized for his "light frivolous music" he was a great popular success from the beginning of his career.

Edvard Grieg (1843-1907) -Norwegian Dance Opus 35, No. 2

See biography above.
Norwegian Dance-besides his music for Henrik Ibsen's Peer Gynt Suite (from which, In the Hall of the Mountain King is extracted), he composed other musical settings for other Norwegian plays, poems, folk songs and dances. Among the dances he wrote is this charming "Norwegian Dance," which he composed for piano in 1870.

Jean-Joseph Mouret (1682-1738) - Rondeau

The name of Jean-Joseph Mouret had virtually disappeared from musical history when the TV series Masterpiece Theater selected it as the main theme for the show. Mouret, a French composer, wrote most of his music in Paris in the early 1700's. His Rondeau (a type of songs of the 13th and 14th centuries) is a movement from one of his popular "divertissements."

Gioacchino Rossini (1792-1868) - William Tell Overture

In 1829, at the age of 37, Rossini (Italian composer) who had recently written some 40 operas was easily the most popular musician in the world. *William Tell*, his last opera, is extremely well known to concert goers of all generations.

Franz Liszt (1811-1886) - Liebestraum

Franz Liszt (Hungarian composer), wildly handsome and hugely talented, cut a wide swath in Paris in the 1830's, where it is said that women actually swooned at his recitals.
Liszt transcribed three of his own songs for piano, calling them "Liebestraume" or "Dreams of Love." The first and most popular in the series is the one here presented.

Contents

Play the Great Masters!

Franz Schubert
MARCHE MILITAIRE

Arr. James Curnow (ASCAP)

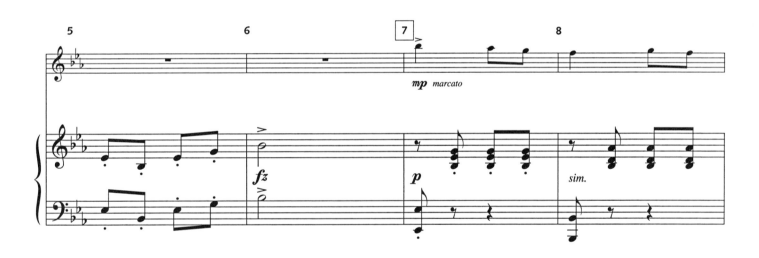

Engelbert Humperdinck
SUITE FROM HANSEL AND GRETEL
Arr. **James Curnow** (ASCAP)

Movement 1.
Evening Prayer

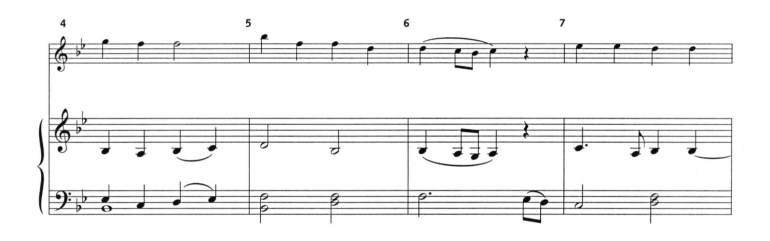

CMP 1069-06

Movement 2.
A Tiny Little Man

SERENADE
Opus 3, No. 5

Franz Joseph Haydn

Arr. **James Curnow** (ASCAP)

SLAVONIC DANCE

Antonin Dvorak

Opus 72, No. 3

Arr. **James Curnow** (ASCAP)

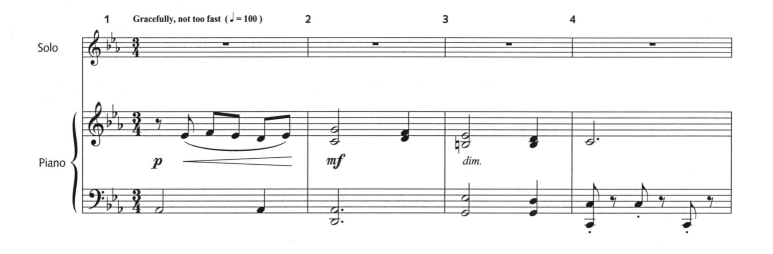

Johannes Brahms
WALTZ

Arr. **James Curnow** (ASCAP)

Edward MacDowell
TO A WILD ROSE

Arr. **James Curnow** (ASCAP)

Pedal harmonically throughout

Franz Schubert
SANCTUS

Arr. **James Curnow** (ASCAP)

Edvard Grieg

IN THE HALL OF THE MOUNTAIN KING

From **Peer Gynt Suite No. 1**

Arr. **James Curnow** (ASCAP)

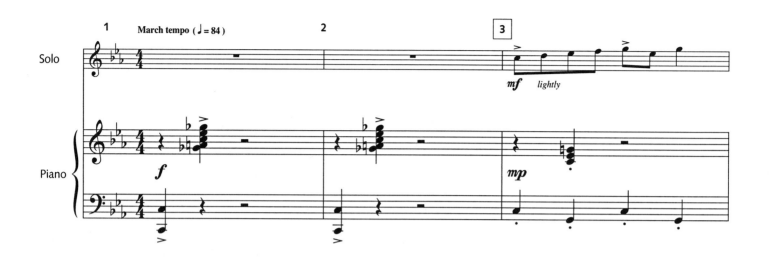

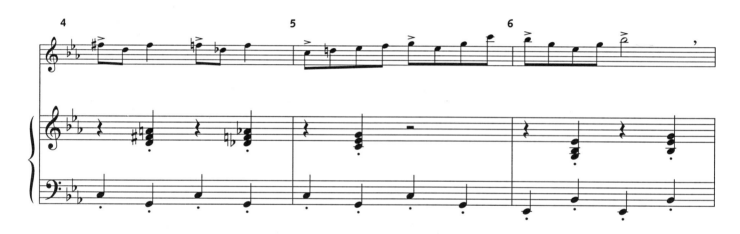

Georges Bizet
HABANERA
From **Carmen**

Arr. **James Curnow** (ASCAP)

Peter Ilych Tchaikovsky (1840 - 1893)
ANDANTE
From **Piano Concerto No. 1**

Arr. **James Curnow** (ASCAP)

Alexander Borodin
Theme from
STRING QUARTET #2
"Nocturne"

Arr. **James Curnow** (ASCAP)

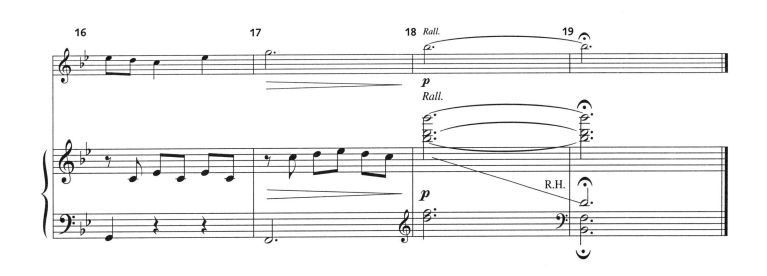

Frederic Chopin
POLONAISE
Op.53

Arr. **James Curnow** (ASCAP)

Johann Strauss, Jr. (1825 - 1899)
THE BLUE DANUBE WALTZ

Arr. **James Curnow** (ASCAP)

Jaques Offenbach (1819-1886)
CAN CAN

Arr. **James Curnow** (ASCAP)

Edvard Grieg
NORWEGIAN DANCE
Opus 35, No. 2

James Curnow (ASCAP)

Jean Joseph Nouret
RONDEAU

Arr. **James Curnow** (ASCAP)

Gioacchino Rossini
WILLIAM TELL OVERTURE

Arr. **James Curnow** (ASCAP)

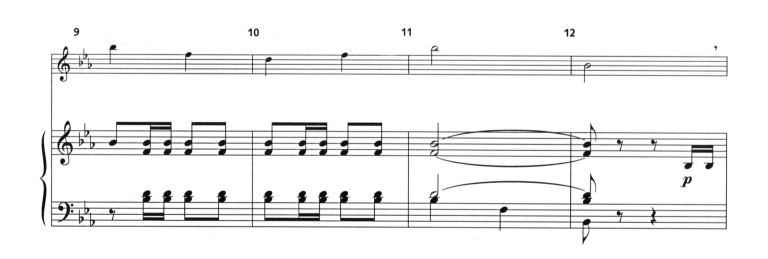

Franz Liszt (1811 - 1886)
LIEBESTRAUM

Arr. **James Curnow** (ASCAP)

Arranged by James Curnow

MEET THE GREAT MASTERS

18 Favorite Classics for Young Players

Contents:

Ludwig van Beethoven – **Ode To Joy**

Robert Schumann – **The Happy Farmer**

George Frederic Handel – **The Harmonious Blacksmith**

Johannes Brahms – **Hungarian Dance #5**

Modest Mussorgsky – **The Great Gate Of Kiev**

Arthur S. Sullivan – **Onward Christian Soldiers**

Antonin Dvorak – **Largo**

Jeremiah Clark – **Trumpet Voluntary**

Franz Joseph Haydn – **Theme From the Emperor Quartet**

Wolfgang Amadeus Mozart – **Theme From Don Juan**

Henry Purcell – **Trumpet Tune**

Felix Mendelssohn – **Hark! the Herald Angels Sing**

Giuseppe Verdi – **Triumphal March**

Johann Sebastian Bach – **Minuet**

Edvard Grieg – **Sailor's Song**

Tylman Susato – **Rondo**

Georges Bizet – **Toreador Song**

Richard Wagner – **Pilgrim's Chorus**

Available for:
Flute/Oboe   CMP 0520-00-400
Clarinet   CMP 0521-00-400
Alto/Baritone Saxophone   CMP 0522-00-400
Soprano/Tenor Saxophone   CMP 0523-00-400
Trumpet   CMP 0525-00-400

F/E♭ Horn   CMP 0526-00-400

Bassoon/Trombone/Euphonium BC/TC   CMP 0524-00-400
Piano Accompaniment   CMP 0527-00-401